DIFFICULT CONVERSATIONS

How to identify, analyze, and deal with bothersome situations on the fly. Apply the best-suited tactics to come out of the battlefield as a winner

KEITH COLEMAN

How to make a killer **First Impression** without embarrassing yourself, even if you're socially awkward and can hardly start a conversation

To sign up for my free author newsletter and get your free copy of the first impressions guidebook *Key Impact*, visit bit.ly/kckeyimpact

TABLE OF CONTENTS

INTRODUCTION

Congratulations on taking a major first step in learning how to handle conflict in a variety of settings.

The following chapters will discuss some of the most
prominent elements of dealing with difficult conversations in all aspects of life such as:

- Meetings in the workplace with co-workers,
  employees and employers alike

- Conversations with children of any age and
  how to keep emotions from running high

- Dealing with difficult situations at home,
  whether it is with a partner or a roommate

- How to handle conflict calmly with friends and with strangers

Regardless of where a conversation takes place, the severity of the topic being covered or how many people are involved, there is always some action that can be taken to ease the situation for everyone, and reach a resolution peacefully. Some of the practiced methods and respected information to be covered include:

- The basics of what makes a difficult conversation so difficult and the elements to focus on when trying to ease into them

- How to identify these situations and plan for them effectively

- Different types of difficult conversations that are common in the workplace and how to approach each most successfully

- How to delegate leadership of a difficult discussion and how to know when the time is right

- And many more professional tips, tricks, and recommendations to help anyone develop the skills they need to master difficult conversations with anyone, anytime and anywhere!

The goal of this book is to provide you with all of the information you could possibly ever need on managing difficult conversations with anyone. Each chapter, word of advice and example was designed to provide you with the ability to create your own personalized toolkit of skills and techniques to use, should a situation arise out of the blue or with ample time to organize.

Chapter 1

GETTING TO KNOW DIFFICULT CONVERSATIONS & HOW TO IDENTIFY THEM

There are four words in the English language that society has learned to dread when heard together, particularly from a supervisor, romantic partner or other close connection: **We need to talk.** No one likes to hear the phrase directed at them because it is always followed up by a difficult conversation that will be:

- Emotionally charged, instigating or frustrating.

- Filled with information that no one wants to hear like bad news or criticism.

- A topic that will inspire changes people are unaware of or not prepared for.

Difficult conversations are unavoidable throughout life whether they happen at work, with close friends or at home with family. Many people across the globe have trouble being the one to start or lead a difficult conversation, and it is rare to find someone who doesn't mind being a part of them (especially those finding themselves in situations where they are a part of regular life such as management or counseling).

While you may not be able to avoid difficult conversations, there are certainly plenty of ways to make them less stressful, painful and emotional for everyone participating. We will be discussing this more in-depth throughout the book, but before getting into the details of various situations that require discussions, it is important to understand more about difficult conversations, why they happen and how to make sure you are prepared before getting involved in one.

WHAT IS A DIFFICULT CONVERSATION?

The specifics to this question are different for everyone, but the most widely accepted definition describes a difficult conversation as one where the topics to be covered, the goals intended to be reached or the issues intended to be resolved have the probability of inspiring a negative emotional response from those involved and creating a sense of anxiety for the one having to initiate or drive the dialogue.

HOW TO IDENTIFY WHEN A DIFFICULT CONVERSATION IS NECESSARY

There are some issues that can be resolved, questions that can be answered and concerns that can be addressed without having to make a fuss and by simply delivering a message or sending an email. Situations like these are when someone has breached protocol on an assignment and needs to make an adjustment, or another small action needs to be taken that won't upset anyone or create tension. This is not the kind of situation management that should be used for:

- Larger concerns that involve a number of people or carry a number of potential consequences.

- Complicated matters that have the potential to create misunderstandings or may need clarification.

- Delicate matters that may concern personal behaviors or emotional responses in an inappropriate environment or circumstance.

- Any situation that needs a direct and particular touch to achieve the desired results and while avoiding exacerbating the state of affairs.

Professional Tip: Build A Set of Rules Based on Proven Techniques

You will find over time that the majority of your rules and guidelines for holding difficult conversations come from gathered experience, but creating a basic "Difficult Conversations Management List" to have on-hand is one of the most passed around and em-braced advice when it comes to learning how to han-dle confrontation or uncomfortable situations no mat-ter where you are or what you're talking about.

Planning an intervention is one of the most common examples of when a person (or group) has decided that the most effective way to communicate their concerns with someone is to invite others that are close to them to take part in a peaceful confrontation in a safe set-ting. The rules for successfully managing interventions are the same for managing any kind of difficult situa-tion. This is something we will cover more deeply in the next chapter as part of the basics of handling diffi-cult conversations anywhere, but some of the best fac-tors to start your personal "Difficult Conversations Management List" with include:

- Researched and proven approaches to a variety of difficult conversations and identifying which one will be the most effective at creating a safe environment.

- Always be welcoming, even if it is a conversation involving negative feedback or addressing problematic conduct.

- Making sure that everyone involved is participating and being heard, but also that everyone is actively listening and interacting.

- Creating a structure for the conversation (what topics are brought up, in what order and establishing how long each person gets to speak without interruption so that everyone has a chance to be heard) and a list of goals you are hoping to achieve.

While having a basic list of guidelines to help with planning and organizing difficult conversations before starting them to simplify the process is a good idea, it will not always have the answers or the methods you need for managing each individual situation. When you run into cases like these, it is important to have the knowledge and patience to make adjustments as needed.

DIFFERENT TYPES OF DIFFICULT CONVERSATIONS

Difficult conversations are a natural part of human interaction which is often unavoidable, each one presenting unique challenges and stresses to those participating. Some of the most common types of difficult conversations include:

Delivering Bad News: This is one of the most dreaded difficult conversations to have in a personal or professional setting. In this type of conversation, you have information that has to be shared with another person, or group of people, that you know is going to upset them. It may be in a small capacity such as disappointment at not meeting a certain goal or in a larger capacity such as having to tell someone about the loss of a family member.

- **Rip Off the Band-Aid:** This is one of the most recommended courses of action for delivering bad news. This doesn't mean being blunt and unempathetic (particularly for conversations that you know will be emotionally charged), but rather to take the initiative and clearly speak when leading the conversation.

  o Don't dance around the topic or put off having the conversation. When it comes to delivering bad news, timing is important. It is always better to compose yourself and control your anxiety over the situation when you find out you have to be the messenger. The sooner you have your own emotions in hand, the more promptly you can plan and conduct the conversation and get it over with for both yourself and the other people involved.

Knowing the Other Person Is Incorrect: This type of difficult conversation is one of the most frustrating anyone can encounter. When someone is incorrect either in actions they've taken or in the information they have but are unwilling to listen or openly communicate with anyone else on the topic, it creates a situation that has little chance of being resolved productively without careful forward motion.

- Also called an oppositional conversation pattern, this type of behavior often has a habit of getting out of hand if not carefully monitored throughout the conversation. In this type of response pattern, the person you are attempting to provide with the correct information refuses to acknowledge their mistake or misunderstanding, regardless of what proof or facts have been provided.

  o More severe cases take it a step further and not only refuse to acknowledge that they are incorrect but make an effort to push their incorrect opinions on the person running the discussion.

- Another important fact to remember about this type of difficult conversation is that there is a difference between disagreeing and discussing.

  o Not everyone is going to agree about every subject or idea brought up during a conversation, and it is important to be open to other opinions (particularly if searching for solutions to complex issues).

  o One way to tell the difference when someone is arguing and when someone is simply voicing a different opinion is that the latter will often lead to some kind of progress, while the former tends to run the conversation in circles with the other person just repeating their stance without listening to what is being said.

- **Choose Your Words Wisely**: The best way to handle this type of difficult conversation is to make sure that, regardless of how the other person speaks or reacts to what is being said, you keep a level tone, a professional attitude and a direct style of dialogue. Choosing the right language is all about understanding the topic that needs to be covered, the setting and tone that are appropriate for the type of conversation, and accepting beforehand that no matter how evenly and patiently you approach the situation you will never be able to fully predict or control how the other person is going to respond.

Requesting A Change in Status or Behavior: This type of conversation is one of the most widely experienced in any industry and environment. Some of the most common examples are parents speaking to a child of any age about a negative behavior like skipping school or supervisors speaking to employees about inappropriate workplace behavior.

- **Listen & Be Supportive:** The best way to handle this type of difficult conversation is to be as open as possible about concerns (without responding emotionally), provide potential solutions instead of just criticizing, and make sure the person you're speaking with knows, not only that they can ask questions throughout the conversation, but that you will also be there to help support their changes or anxieties when the discussion is over.

QUESTIONS TO ASK BEFORE GETTING INVOLVED IN A DIFFICULT CONVERSATION

Whether you are the one initiating it, in charge of leading it or were invited as a participant, there are some questions that are important to have a definitive answer to before getting entangled in a difficult conversation.

- What am I hoping to accomplish with the dialogue established in this conversation?

  o This question is important for those managing difficult conversations to know before starting because it is the best way to track progress and maintain focus should emotions start to run high and those participating get off topic.

  o This is important for those who are just acting as participants in difficult conversations to ask themselves as well because it can help with determining how to voice your opinions and what questions to ask throughout the conversation.

    ▪ This may not always be possible if the conversation was announced without warning or the topic was not advertised in the invitation (whether that was written or verbal).

- Don't ever be afraid to ask about the subject and goals of the conversation when you become aware of it and for a few minutes to gather your thoughts before the scheduled time.

- How safe and welcomed do you feel with regards to the setting, timing and other people involved in the conversation?

  o If you are feeling uncomfortable about where, when or how the conversation has been organized, then it is important to speak up. After all, the main point of any difficult conversation is to encourage open communication.

    - The chances are, if you're feeling uncomfortable, then others are as well. When people are uncomfortable, they are less likely to share their opinions openly and honestly.

- Based on past experience, how well do you think you will be able to control your emotions during this conversation?

  o Are there any actions you can take before the conversation to ensure a calmer frame of mind for yourself?

  o If it is a sensitive subject being discussed, can you approach the conversation with an open mind and avoid getting defensive when others share differing opinions or critical comments?

- Are you in the right mental and emotional state to participate in this conversation?

  o Being in the right frame of mind before starting a difficult conversation is critical because it can affect a number of factors including how productive the meeting will be, how you will react when others become emotional and how active you will be throughout the conversation.

Professional Tip: Don't Be Afraid to Delegate, But Know When It's Necessary

Difficult conversations are emotional experiences, no matter how hard those in charge try to keep everyone calm and focused. No matter how long you have to prepare, how prepared you are beforehand, or how experienced you are with different types of difficult conversations, there may be situations or topics of discussion that you are not the most qualified to handle. In situations like these, it is crucial to find the right person for the job and help prepare them for having to be the one to lead the conversation in your place.

While delegating is a valuable skill to practice (particularly in professional or business settings), it is important to remember that there is a difference between delegating a task and avoiding one. If you're someone that doesn't handle conflict well or gets emotional easily, it can be tempting to put someone else in charge. However, this is an unhealthy response to stressful situations and can lead to larger communication issues if abused as a regular practice.

Here are some questions to ask before delegating a difficult conversation to someone else:

- Why am I delegating this conversation?

    o For some, the answer may be that they do not have the right knowledge or information about the topic or goals of the conversation. Others may need to delegate because of their existing relationship or history with the other person or people involved.

    o Inability to get control of one's emotions and fear of confrontation are not reasons to delegate leadership of a difficult conversation. If these (or similar reasons) are what you come up with when asking the question, then instead of delegating the task, it would be healthier for you and the others involved in the conversation to find a way to come together peacefully and agree to communicate openly.

- Is the person I'm delegating this to qualified to manage it to the desired outcome?

  o Before handing over control of a situation to someone else, it is good to be aware of their individual skills and how they can be used to effectively reach goals and cover topics that need to be discussed in the specific situation.

- What can I do to make sure the person I'm delegating this to is fully prepared?

  o If you are unable to manage the conversation yourself, it is most effective (and only right) to make sure that the person taking your place is as ready as they can be for any issues that may arise or any questions that may come up.

o One of the best ways to do this is to make sure to have an in-person meeting about the conversation, the resolution you are hoping for and any predictable factors that may affect how successful the conversation will be. While it may be easier to send an email or speak over the phone, meeting face-to-face builds confidence in both parties about how the conversation is planned to play out, allows both parties to ask questions if there is anything that is unclear or misunderstood from earlier communications, and provides a number of other benefits that can only come from meeting in person.

o Not every difficult conversation will be preceded by a time frame long enough to allow for this. In these cases, the best way to move forward is to make sure you are able to be contacted by the person left in charge at any time during the conversation for questions or to communicate concerns. This could mean answering emails or texts sent during the conversation or checking in with the delegated leader during scheduled breaks throughout the course of the meeting.

Now that you have a better idea of what kinds of situations require difficult conversations and how to identify and approach them, we'll get more in detail about the Basics of Difficult Conversations and how to stop seeing them as daily stress factors, but rather powerful communication tools that can benefit everyone involved!

Chapter 2

THE BASICS OF HANDLING DIFFICULT CONVERSATIONS ANYWHERE

Every difficult conversation is going to require its own tools, patience, and adjustments to get through and reach the intended goals, but there are some skills and practices that can be used as a basis for handling difficult conversations that may come up anywhere, unexpectedly or with time prepare.

The best way to handle difficult conversations successfully and without incident is to make sure to have the basic skills necessary to do so. Many people develop these skills at work or school as they are promoted to take charge of other employees or lead teams of their peers to meet specific goals. This is not always the case though, so it falls to team leaders and managers who struggle with difficult conversations to take the initiative and develop their own skill set to have on call when situations arise.

In this chapter, we'll take a closer look at some of the most effective techniques in use over a variety of industries and settings across the globe.

Professional Tip: Bite the Bullet & Get It Done

Difficult conversations are never something to look forward to but putting them off (for better circumstances, timing or other excuses) creates more problems than it solves.

There are a number of reasons people try to avoid difficult conversations, mostly it is a tempting option for those who have trouble controlling their emotional responses or are overwhelmed by anxiety at the thought of delivering bad news or criticism. It is critical to keep in mind that any time you avoid an issue, it is only a temporary answer to a problem that is going stay in the shadows and intensify the longer it is left unmanaged.

WHY WOULD SOMEONE WANT TO AVOID AN IMPORTANT CONVERSATION?

It is an easy question to ask from an outside perspective. When we are not the ones having to manage or take part in the actual conversation, most people would wonder what the appeal is of evading the situation instead of just getting it out of the way, so they don't have to think about it anymore.

However, the reality is that most people would rather avoid dealing with complex situations (hoping instead that they will resolve themselves) than just collect their thoughts and get the conversations over with. This is an unhealthy response to stress that is widely practiced (often unintentionally as an unconscious psychological reaction) by people around the world for a range of reasons including:

- Negative experiences with previous difficult conversations that left an emotional mark.

- Not having the proper training or experience to successfully deal with difficult conversations without causing drama or creating more problems.

- Working or living in an environment that does not encourage direct conversations, opting instead for passive communication like sending emails or texts, leaving messages or sending someone else with a message.

THE NEGATIVE EFFECTS OF AVOIDING CONFRONTATION & DIFFICULT CONVERSATIONS

9 times out of 10 a difficult situation will not resolve itself over time, instead of worsening and becoming more poisonous to the environment and everyone

around. Some of the most common negative effects of avoiding having difficult conversations include:

- Loss of respect for leaders whose employees, students or co-workers look to them to take charge, but see them being passive-aggressive instead.

- Waste of valuable time (particularly in professional settings) as so much energy is spent avoiding the conversation that little else gets accomplished.

- Tiptoeing around difficult conversations increases personal stress and can lead to the development of psychological issues that can spread to affect other aspects of life.

  o One of the most common negative effects of avoiding confrontation is projecting emotions on others where it is not only unnecessary but also inappropriate.

- People who take their work stress home and find themselves arguing with or avoiding spending time with their family are often suffering from emotional projection.

- Here are some ideas for those wanting to break themselves of this habit and get on the path to mastering difficult conversations:

  o Don't be afraid to ask for help! Choose someone you trust to be an accountability partner.

    - Accountability partners are a powerful tool most commonly used by those looking to get over an addiction or recover from a negative experience where they need extra support.

    - Basically, this person will be responsible for making sure that when there are difficult conversations to have or stressful situations that fall to you to manage, you do so in a timely and effective manner.

o   Have a list of topics that need to be covered to keep you on track should the situation start to become emotional.

o   Focus on building trust with those you have difficult conversations with regularly such as co-workers or children. The more you are trusted by those you have to speak with, the calmer the process will be, the more that will be accomplished and the less dreaded these conversations become over time as positive connections are made through experience.

When it comes down to it, it is always better to just have the conversations and deal the with situations when they come up or as quickly as possible before they have a chance to worsen and become a condition that needs outside attention or that can't be dealt with without heightened emotions, further complicating the issue.

GETTING THINGS STARTED: SETTING YOURSELF UP FOR SUCCESS

Starting a difficult conversation is often the most trying part of dealing with these situations. Everyone has their limits and finds different aspects of conversations to be the worst part of having to have them. For some, difficult conversations are easier when they have to be had with someone they know well, while others find it harder to speak frankly with their friends or family. Knowing how to approach conversations with anyone, anywhere and about anything is the best way to conquer anxieties or dread that comes with all of life's surprises.

Whether you've had time to prepare or it's something that needs to be dealt with unexpectedly, but efficiently, there are ways to initiate a difficult conversation to ease pain, stress, and panic for both sides. Here is a closer look at some of the best first steps to take if you find yourself having to be the one to break bad news, give criticism or be the driver of any kind of difficult conversation.

Make Sure to Set It Up Right: The initial approach taken by the principal speaker can also be the determining factor for how successful a conversation will be from start to finish. This is why it is so important to begin difficult conversations the correct way to ensure that neither party is going to get over-emotional or defensive.

- **Establish A Connection**: Finding some common ground is often the best way to start any kind of conversation. This is particularly useful for setting up conversations with children or with someone you have a personal connection with like a friend or a romantic partner. Some ideas for establishing a connection include:

o Planning an activity such as taking a walk or meeting somewhere like a coffee shop can create a sense of comfort for all parties involved and also keep involved parties from forming negative emotional connections to daily visited or regular surroundings.

o If it is a conversation with the potential to require more than one meeting, either find a regular place and time to meet up (planned out before or during the first meeting) or use knowledge and information gathered during each individual meeting to create more personalized experiences or more amiable time frames.

- **Set Up Ground Rules:** This is particularly important for difficult conversations where one person has the correct information, and the other participants (whether it is one person or a group of them) are refusing to accept or are unaware that they are incorrect. This is also a useful step for those who are conversing with someone they already know tends to react emotionally or impulsively. Ground rules can be established for any number of reasons, and many people already have a basic list they have created through experience, that can be used as a basis for handling a variety of difficult situations. However, there is always the possibility that these rules need to be adjusted depending on the specifics of the situation, the people involved, where the conversation is taking place and any number of other factors.

o   Setting time limits for meetings and conversations is one ground rule set by successful leaders and managers. When topics or ideas need to be discussed over a number of meetings or with different people, having time limits has its benefits including:

- Keeping everyone on topic and focused on the important aspects of the conversation.

- Within the limits of the meeting, everyone can plan to have a set amount of time to speak. This keeps one person of the pair or group from commandeering the conversation and making everyone involved feel as though they're equals.

- A common time limit is half an hour to an hour per meeting. This keeps people from getting over-exhausted or letting the conversation run in circles.

o Another popular ground rule widely used for managing difficult conversations is taking turns speaking. This keeps extroverts or emotional speakers from dominating conversations and ensures that more introverted, stubborn or disconnected participants not only have a chance to speak but know that they must.

- **Establish Reasonable Goals:** Having established goals going into a difficult conversation can help with encouraging progress, maintaining focus and letting everyone involved know that there is a solid purpose for the current situation, and real consequences should the conversation not take place or be interrupted.

  o For those who go into a conversation knowing it is going to take more than one meeting, set one or two goals for each meeting and adjust from there depending on how the conversation goes each time.

  o For those who go into a conversation with one or two clear goals that have to be discussed within one meeting, make sure to address them clearly and openly at the start of the conversation so that everyone knows what needs to be covered in the time that you have.

Show Appreciation & Make Participants Feel Welcomed: Whether it is just one meeting or several, everyone wants to feel like their time has been well spent. One way to set up a difficult conversation and keep everyone feeling significant throughout the process is to thank those involved for contributing their time, opinions, information and participation.

- **Be Inviting:** When starting a difficult conversation with someone or with a group, make sure that everyone involved knows that they play an important role in the process and that coming to a solution is a team effort. Let everyone know they are there to not only listen but to be heard. This makes people feel welcomed and more comfortable. Comfortable people are easier to communicate openly and effectively with, making difficult conversations easier and more proficient.

- **A Little Thankfulness Goes A Long Way:** This is especially true for difficult conversations that require all parties involved to come to an agreement or a solution. Sometimes this isn't as complicated as people are expecting it to be and solutions can come easily. However, more often than not (particularly in professional settings), the reason the difficult conversation is having to be held in the first place, is because the resolutions are complicated, and communication is gridlocked.

  o Thank people for their time, their readiness to share their thoughts and feelings, and their commitment to listening to what's be-

ing said, even if it is information or complications they do not want to hear about.

o   Being thanked for making the effort to un-
dertake a difficult conversation helps to
build people's confidence in their own
voice, makes it easier to get them to be
more open about what's on their mind in
future conversations, and creates a positive
emotional connection with communi-
cating that benefits not only the person
who initiated the conversation but also everyone who got involved.

**Control the Tone Throughout & End on A Positive
Note:** Not every meeting and conversation is going to
be as productive or effective as everyone hopes. The
human factors like emotional responses, scheduling
conflicts, and other elements can be monitored but
never fully controlled. This is why it is important to
centralize the party's focus on and applaud all of the

progress made during the meeting, instead of being held back by negative factors that may have hindered how productive everyone was at reaching the established goals.

ALWAYS REVIEW THE CONVERSATION BEFORE WRAPPING THINGS UP

Often at the end of a difficult conversation, the only thing people can think about is getting out of there and thinking about anything other than their current situation. However, it is always a good idea to save at least five minutes of the allotted meeting time for a review of what was covered and what was accomplished, or not accomplished depending on how the conversation has progressed. This gets everyone on the same page before going their separate ways, ensures there isn't any misunderstanding that could be harmful to any forward progress made and gives the conversation leader a chance to thank everyone for their time, and encourage open communication in the days that follow so that these conversations are fewer and farther between.

There are a number of benefits to having a review before ending a difficult conversation regardless of where, when or with who it takes place.

- Reviews give everyone one last chance to ask questions or ask for clarification on anything they may be confused about.

- They also provide an opportunity to assess where the situation the conversation focused on stands before everyone goes their separate ways.

  o This is a chance to track progress made in the meeting, make a note of what wasn't covered or covered as well as it needed to be, and plan out what needs to be discussed in the next meeting or conversation (if one is required).

- Reviews provide an opportunity to make a note of the most important topics, comments, decisions or responses discussed during the meeting for an easier time preparing for future meetings.

REFLECT ON & LEARN FROM EVERY DIFFICULT CONVERSATION YOU HAVE

Not every conversation is going to be a successful one, but every conversation is a chance to learn from the experience to help improve future discussions. Personal reflection is an important part of everyday life and a good skill to develop as part of your daily routine if you don't already. Many people like to do their personal daily reflection in bed as they ease into sleep, others save it for their daily meditating, or to think about while they're exercising. Whatever time works best for your daily schedule is the perfect time to take a moment to reflect.

Professional Tip: Keep A Journal

Whether your difficult conversations happen more often at work or in personal settings, having a reviewable record of thoughts and reflections that dominated your mind in the hours before and following the conversation can help with:

- Being more emotionally prepared for the next conversation or meeting by having a record of how your emotions changed before, during and after the experience.

- Being more knowledgeable and informed for future difficult conversations that may relate to the one you've just been through (or that are unrelated but have similar goals) by having notes to look back on.

- Journals can also be where you take your notes during the meeting in order to reflect on them later. This gives you the opportunity to list concerns to look into, thoughts you would like to develop further or questions you had about the topic or goals covered in the meeting (whether you are in charge of the conversation or acting as a participant).

A journal can become the center of your daily reflection, or it can be a tool used specifically for recording your thoughts and feelings about difficult situations you're experiencing or find yourself in charge of handling. The timing is not as important as just getting into the habit. This is an especially helpful option for those who feel as though they have no one to talk to about their thoughts and feelings on certain topics. Writing them out without worrying about negative reactions that can happen can help with building confidence in those that have difficulty expressing themselves in conversations, or around people they have to see on a daily basis.

QUESTIONS TO ASK WHEN REFLECTING ON A DIFFICULT CONVERSATION

- How do I feel about the conversation and how it progressed?

  o This question helps you reflect on the event itself like how everyone behaved, what progress was made, where the hold-ups were and any ideas on how to help improve these elements during your next conversation

- How do you feel about your behavior before, during and after the conversation?

  o Did you have any emotional outbursts or reactions that could have been avoided or controlled?

  o How active were you in the conversation? Did you ask any questions or share any opinions?

- How do you feel about the topic of the difficult conversation now compared to before the meeting?

  o Have your thoughts or feelings changed? Was the change positive or negative?

- What could have been changed or eliminated to improve the experience or progress for everyone who participated in the talk?

  o Could the meeting have been held in a better place? Was the length okay or should it be altered to increase productivity for the next conversation?

  o Should someone else have led the meeting or someone else have been included to enhance the experience?

- What did you learn from the experience and how can it be used to help decrease the stress or complication of future conversations you may face?

When it comes down to it, the more driven you are to developing the skills and collecting the tools needed to master difficult conversations, the easier and less stressful they will become over time. This collection of techniques and methods can be personalized to meet the specific requirements of difficult conversations you have to have as a part of your daily life. Keep reading to learn more about difficult conversations in different settings and with different purposes in the chapters that follow and become a master at handling any issues that present themselves in a timely and effective manner!

Chapter 3

THE INS & OUTS OF MANAGING DIFFICULT CONVERSATIONS AT WORK

Difficult conversations aren't fun to have anywhere, but most people find that these situations tend to pop up both out of the house or in the workplace. Open communication is one of the most influential factors needed to be maintained in order to keep a team and a business running smoothly. Unfortunately, this maintenance often requires holding meetings or private conversations with fellow employees of all levels that address concerns or behaviors that are problematic to the productivity of the office or workspace.

In this chapter, we will cover some of the most practiced and proven techniques for handling difficult conversations at work to everyone's mutual satisfaction and benefit.

THE BASICS OF MANAGING DIFFICULT CONVERSATIONS WITH CO-WORKERS

Some people find that discussions with co-workers are the least stressful types of difficult conversations in the workplace; others will admit that they are the most dreaded. When everyone is on the same team and shares the same responsibilities without one person having more influence than the others (like a manager or CEO) tensions can start to grow from the slightest actions like a misunderstood intention or incorrect statement. No one needs to panic or dread these types of conversations as long as they know how to handle them and move forward without distress.

Acknowledge Everyone & Even the Field: Speaking with co-workers can often be a delicate task. After all, these are people that you see, speak to and work with on a regular basis and have to maintain a semblance of civility with. These are also people who you are most likely on the same level with professionally, your peers, people you trust to have your back on the job. This is why it is good to keep in mind during conversations with co-workers that listening and empathizing are just as important as speaking openly about your ideas or concerns. Everyone needs to feel valued and respected in order for communication to flow naturally and productively.

- Don't announce the need for a conversation or try to boss your co-workers around. A better approach is to request their involvement in a difficult conversation and invite them to share their thoughts on the matter.

  o This lets you know who is most concerned with the subject to be covered in the conversation, who is most actively involved in the team and who is not.

o The people who do not attend may have any number of reasons for doing so such as disinterest or lack of knowledge in the subject, personal problems with other co-workers that keeps them from participating, or concerns with the job, assignment or company in general that they do not feel comfortable speaking on with the whole team. For situations like this, the best way to manage it is to have the conversation as planed with those who attend and then speak to those who did not attend on a one-on-one basis. This creates a safe environment that encourages reluctant co-workers to be more open.

• Make sure to show everyone that you appreciate them taking the time to have the conversation and invite them to share their thoughts and feelings throughout.

- Remind everyone that their opinions matter and make sure to stay on top of when people are interrupting others or speaking negatively to one another.

- Don't be afraid to remind everyone that you are a team and that when the team works together, everyone has an easier time, and work gets done without clashing. One trick to doing this is avoiding using words like "you" when addressing the team or the other person and focus on structuring the conversation around "we" statements:

  o We need to come up with solutions to this issue

  o We need to focus on this assignment as a priority

- o *We* should always communicate openly and professionally

Be Relatable & Focus On the Facts: One way to keep emotions from escalating during a difficult conversation with co-workers is to make sure that all of the information you're sharing, concerns you're addressing and options you're laying out are based on facts and can be backed up with numbers, quotes or experience should anyone get upset by or react emotionally to what is being discussed. This protects you from any kind of backlash should someone take issue with any part of the conversation and react with a complaint or with tension in the workplace.

For those who are laying out the details of a specific situation, make sure that your co-workers are able to relate to everything you're saying. If there are some people in the group who haven't been trained on a certain task or are new to the team, make sure to keep the conversation basic and open for discussion if there are questions.

Know What the Next Step Is: The answer to this will be different for each unique situation, but as an employee speaking and forming solutions with co-workers, it is most likely that the actual enacting of those solutions and changes will fall to a higher level employee (like a team leader or supervisor) after all of the information gathered at the meetings has been passed along. Knowing what is going to be done with the answers and resolutions that are fashioned during the conversation is good to find out when you are assigned the task of leading it. It is most likely a question that will come up during the discussion and it also helps with determining how productive the meeting was by setting a bar for what needs to be completed.

THE GOLDEN RULES OF HANDLING DIFFICULT CONVERSATIONS AS AN EMPLOYEE TALKING TO A SUPERVISOR

Making a request of or speaking about a serious subject with your boss is rarely something people look forward to and can be a cause of great stress for many employees (especially those with challenging supervisors). Following these simple tips for how to approach and speak with your boss and success will be in your grasp!

Have A Plan Going In: Before you even approach an employer about concerns or requests it is important to know what you are going to say, how you want to express yourself, and what the plan is for moving forward once the conversation is completed.

- Anticipate questions your employer will ask and concerns they may have with the topic you are hoping to cover and decide how you will respond. This is an important part of the preparation as it shows your employer that you have the foresight to plan and also have the ability to take the initiative when there is a problem that needs to be solved.

o   This skill helps not only with the situation, but it also has the potential to improve your standing and position with the business by demonstrating positive elements to your work personality and drawing attention to your range of valuable skills.

- Know your specific objectives and have action-able solutions in mind for resolving the situation to both yours and your employer's satisfaction.

  o   This improves your chances of a positive outcome because it shows you've already done most of the work and at this point, all you need is approval or support.

Choose the Right Setting: The right time and place can help with setting the tone for the conversation and reaching the desired results. It is important to take into consideration for organizing any kind of serious conversation, but it is even more so for conversations with supervisors and team leaders as they often have the ability to affect your standing within the company.

- Always make sure to request a meeting in person and schedule it ahead of time. Springing issues or serious requests on employers can have a negative effect on how successful your pitch or discussion will be before you ever get to actually have the conversation.

- Be tactful and respectful, especially with delicate or private subjects. Even if your issue is with the employer you're speaking to, maintain a professional tone and stick to the important factors. This shows that you mean business and are not reacting out of emotional distress connected to the topic you're bringing up.

- Never approach them in front of other employees, whether they are other supervisors or other employees, especially when bringing up private or sensitive matters. This creates an awkward situation for everyone present, espe-cially if the conversation is based around work-place conflict.

Once you have requested the meeting and set up the time and place, the next step is to make sure to express yourself clearly, make practical requests and keep communication open. Make sure to ask their thoughts and concerns on the matter and be patient with any questions they may have during the conversation.

DIFFICULT CONVERSATIONS FOR EMPLOYEES & EMPLOY-ERS: ASKING FOR A PAY INCREASE

The main reason people get out of bed each day and go to their place of employ is the pay that comes from the work they put in, regardless of what the specifics of their job may be. Eventually, as employees gather more experience, develop more advanced skills, suc-cessfully accomplish major undertakings and show their loyalty to the business by just being there for an extended period of time, all employees want to be rewarded with an increase in their individual pay.

Those who have an issue with conflict may prefer just to wait until raises are offered, but if the company does not have a set pay increase schedule or policies in place, there is little to no guarantee of that ever occurring without a nudge in the right direction. For those with the knowledge and skills to effectively approach their supervisors to ask for a raise, this can be a stress-free and even pleasant experience that helps with building confidence and practicing valuable communication abilities.

First Step: Do your research and your preparation before even bringing up wanting to speak with your boss. Answer the following questions as part of your planning:

- Why am I asking for this pay increase? When was my last one?

- What are the company's policies on giving out raises? Who should I speak to about getting that information?

  o The answer to the latter question is usually the Human Resources department. Be careful about how much information you share with them when researching the company's pay raise policies as you don't want word of your intentions reaching your employer before you've had a chance to make your proposal.

- What recent behaviors, accomplishments or changes have I been a part of that could be used as a means of support for my pay increase request?

  o It is much easier to convince your employer that a pay increase is due if you have specific proof and examples of how valuable you are to the team and the business.

Second Step: Timing is everything when it comes to requesting more money, so it is important to plan your approach and schedule your conversation during amiable windows. Every company has times when their business is at its peak, and while this is a good time for employees to prove their worth, these are also the times when supervisors and employers tend to be at their busiest and most stressed out. The more distracted an employer is, the more burnt out or in demand they feel, the more likely you are to be turned down or pushed to the back burner and told to come back later.

The best times to approach your supervisor about how to get a pay increase are:

- After making a notable achievement that benefits the team or company in a way that should be recognized like closing a big account or exceeding an established sales goal.

- After being with the company for a set amount of time. One way to determine if enough time has passed is to look at the company's regular turnover rate. For example, if you've been with the company for three to five years, this can be seen as a major feat for companies that see employees coming in and out after a few months to a year, and the timing could be perfect for requesting a pay increase. However, if you work for a company where the average worker is there for five to seven years the timing may not be right, and you should prepare yourself for arguments your employer could make for having you wait some more time before increasing your pay rate.

- After gathering more skills and training. It's only reasonable that the more experience you gather, the more pay you should receive. This is because those who are more experienced or who have received more training may receive more responsibilities and are held to higher standards than their co-workers who only have the basic skills needed for their position.

- If you have gone above and beyond your job description such as regularly taking on extra assignments, being put in charge of helping others on the team, training new employees on a consistent basis. As long as you can show your work and provide examples, there should be no reason for getting denied a pay increase.

Finally: Make sure that your request is reasonable, and still be prepared to negotiate, regardless of how prepared you are going into the meeting and how much support you have for why you deserve the raise. It may not sound fair, but even the best salespeople have to be ready to accept less than they request when trying to land a sale. Negotiation is a natural part of the business world and another valuable skill everyone should try to develop throughout their career. A smaller pay increase is still better than treading water in your current situation and also gives you an idea of what to expect the next time an opportunity to request a pay increase presents itself.

HOW TO HAVE DIFFICULT CONVERSATIONS WITH EMPLOY-EES AS A MANAGER OR SUPERVISOR

Handling difficult situations is an expected part of moving up to management or accepting any kind of leadership position. While you may already have a good idea of the tools needed to do this, learning through experience is the most recommended means of training in industries across the globe. Here is a closer look at some of the simple rules leaders can follow when having to bring up a difficult topic like disappointing performance or potentially awkward subjects like inappropriate behavior or conduct.

- **Keep the Conversation Balanced**: Difficult conversations are most often sparked by or filled with negative thoughts, concerns or comments. This knowledge puts everyone in-volved in the situation, into a defensive frame of mind that means little progress or waste of time due to uncontrolled emotional reactions.

o   The best way to keep this from becoming a problem is to make sure that there is enough positive information being dis-cussed to balance out the negativity.

o   For meetings where employee perfor-mance is being criticized, make sure to fo-cus on actionable solutions to encourage improvement instead of just listing cri-tiques. It is also a good idea to make sure you acknowledge the positive work the employee or employees are doing and make them feel appreciated.

- **Pros & Cons:** Make sure that the employee is not only aware of what needs to change or be corrected, but also that they know the difficulties that will come with adjustment and the benefits they will see once the changes have been made such as opening lines of communication to ease workflow or taking some extra training courses to simplify the work the employee is responsible for.

- **Don't Just Leave It**: The relief felt at the end of a difficult conversation is often enough to have everyone involved feel more positively about what was discussed and what was decided. This is not enough to ensure the complete success of the discussion, and therefore it is important to always review the conversation before breaking the meeting to make sure that everyone is on the same page and understands what the next steps are. Once that is done, all leaders should check-in regularly with the employees spoken to just to make sure that the issue has been resolved whether that is improving overall performance or changing a certain behavior.

Professional Tip: Embrace Role Play as A Practical Means of Preparation

Before approaching an employee, employer or groups of team members with a difficult subject, you should have already designed a plan of action for how to proceed with the conversation and know what you want to speak about and what you want to achieve. This may not be enough to boost your confidence high enough that you are ready to face the situation without additional anticipation stress or anxiety. One of the best solutions to this issue is to try role-playing, an exercise that allows people to practice their plans or speeches ahead of time to help improve the conversation's direction and flow while also identifying complications that may come up during the actual discussion.

It is important when role-playing to ask someone you trust and whose opinion you respect to help you. This ensures that rumors about the conversation will not spread around the workplace before you have a chance to speak with everyone involved personally or announce the meeting yourself. Some people like to find a third-party helper that is not related to or affected by the subject of the conversation. This takes some of the risks out of sharing information before you're ready. Others prefer to recruit someone who is knowledgeable about the topic already, so they can ask questions or raise concerns more effectively while you practice your plan of action. It all comes down to personal preference and experience.

Regardless of your level and experience, the main rule to focus on when planning out difficult conversations in the workplace is that everyone wants to be treated with respect and feel as though they are a valued member of the business.

- Speak directly, but not offensively.

- Explain subjects and ideas clearly, but do not patronize.

- Be patient and open to outside opinions, but do not let anyone force their thoughts or feelings on others.

Follow these simple guidelines and put them into practice in all aspects of your life. The more you work on developing the skills needed to handle difficult situations in the workplace, the more successful you will be throughout your career!

Chapter 4

HOW TO HANDLE DIFFICULT CONVERSATIONS AT HOME

Having difficult conversations at home with family or roommates can be some of the most dreaded that any person will face throughout their lifetime. Home is supposed to be a safe environment where we can relax and forget about the stresses of the outside world. When those stresses start to seep into our home lives, it creates an awkward and often painful setting where no one can relax or live confidently because of unspoken questions or concerns that are bubbling away without resolution. The longer these concerns are allowed to remain unaddressed, the more poisonous the environment becomes until any kind of solution begins to feel impossible.

However, if dealt with in a timely manner and with the right kind of approach, concerns and issues in the home do not have to be a matter of anxiety and strain. This chapter covers some of the most effective and tested methods of dealing with at-home conflicts in a way that brings peace and comfort to everyone living there.

HOW TO TACKLE DIFFICULT CONVERSATIONS WITH YOUR SPOUSE OR PARTNER

When you've decided to spend your life with someone, you have signed on for the good situations and the bad (both of which are inevitable throughout the course of a relationship). Having to address issues or concerns is uncomfortable anywhere, but it can be even worse to think about having to have difficult conversations with your spouse or partner. Like with any negative situations that need to be addressed, avoiding it is only going to make things worse, so it is critical to be direct and handle the discussion in a timely manner instead of letting negative emotions or hurtful thoughts fester.

Here is a closer look at some of the most widely practiced methods for managing conversations with your romantic partner in a way that helps settle problems and restores peace to your home.

- **Always Look Toward the Future:** One of the most common reasons couples end up seeking professional assistance or just calling it quits is because one or both of the pair are unable to move forward from difficult conversations and uncomfortable situations.

  - Dwelling in the past is a dangerous habit for individuals and all relationships throughout their life be it with family, lovers or friends.

o One of the easiest ways to break yourself or help break your partner this habit is to make sure that every difficult conversation you have not only covers problems and concerns but also creates solutions or makes decisions on steps moving forward.

o Practice optimism, forgiveness, empathy, and understanding. These skills are central to setting yourself and your spouse/partner up for a successful relationship that both of you can feel confident in, even during the tough times.

- **Listen & Compromise:** Be ready (and willing) to make concessions from time to time. In a relationship, it is more important to find a way to meet halfway and agree on solutions than it is to convince your spouse/partner that your ideas are the only way to go. Dealing with difficult situations in the home is not a competition, but it can often feel that way due to the high level of emotions and how much easier it is to get defensive when having to face confrontation in your own living space.

o   This does not mean just agreeing to everything that's said in order to avoid emotional outbursts or stressful discussions. Compromise is about both of you voicing your thoughts and ideas about a topic or problem. This way you are aware of where each other stands before working together to choose the best course of action or solution for the situation.

• **Accept Natural Human Behavior as Unavoidable**: No matter how calmly you start a conversation or how well prepared you are, there is no way to fully predict how you or your spouse/partner is going to react to what is said. Accepting that as inevitable before getting involved in emotionally charged discussions will help you with patience, listening, and not torturing yourself over emotional changes, especially if they end up affecting your behavior.

o   This is also part of always looking forward. Not every conversation is going to go as planned and there will be times when there is an interruption or development that throws the plan off the rails, leading to a decided failure.

o   Instead of obsessing over these situations, reflect on them to see what incited them and determine what could have been done to prevent or recover from them. Once that is done, use it as a learning experience and focus your thoughts on how you can reintroduce the conversation topic in a way that will be more successful.

Professional Tip: Ditch the Good News/Bad News Conversation Style

In order to keep people's feelings from being hurt, or to lessen the chances of them having a negative emotional reaction to a statement they won't want to hear, a popular discussion method involves easing them into the bad news statement by starting with something that is positive.

For example, one party rearranged the kitchen while the other was at work (dishes, food storage, countertop devices) without consulting the other person who came home and found themselves lost in their own kitchen. It is a small situation that could easily be cleared up with a quick and open conversation about why they were upset by the change. However, the other partner is proud of the changes they made and likes the new arrangement. The partner initiating the conversation is worried about making them upset and now have several paths to choose from on how best to approach the situation without making things worse.

1. Ignore their personal concerns and feelings about it, hoping the situation will resolve itself.

   - If they feel like they are over-reacting and want to take a few days to get accustomed to the changes then taking a breath may be their best option to begin with.

   - If it is not the changes themselves and the fact that a decision on how the house was changed without even a warning, then this is not the action to take as avoiding confrontation to spare someone's feelings only leads to more conflict and struggle.

2. Take a few minutes to collect their thoughts instead of reacting immediately and impulsively before speaking with their partner about what happened.

- This path gives them the opportunity to collect their thoughts and determine why exactly they are upset before confronting their partner about the issue at hand.

3. Try to minimize how the conflict has affected them by not voicing their true thoughts and offering up a Good News/Bad News statement like:

- It's great that you're taking an interest in making the house feel more home-like, but...

- I like the way you've moved everything around, but...

- The kitchen looks great, but...

While this style of conversation may seem like a good way to lessen the blow when voicing an unpopular opinion or delivering bad news, but in reality, it is a temporary fix that creates more issues over time than it solves. You can be honest about the positive aspects of the situation. It is widely encouraged to balance out negative comments with positive ones, but this is not the way to go about it (especially when speaking to people you have an emotional connection to like partners, friends or children). When experienced on a regular basis, this style of discussion teaches people to dread receiving positive news or compliments because they have learned that positive statements can often be followed by negative ones that often turn out the be the true reason for a conversation to begin with.

This is why it is recommended by professionals, psychologists and researchers alike to be as straightforward and direct as possible when having difficult conversations in the home or anywhere with people you love. This doesn't suggest to be mean about problems when bringing them up. Always remain civil and empathetic, but unemotional, focusing on facts and questions rather than verbally attacking them or storming off.

HOW TO HANDLE CONVERSATIONS WITH A DIFFICULT ROOMMATE

Initiating difficult conversations with roommates can be complex and awkward, depending on how close you are with the person you're living with. Some people say that difficult conversations with roommates are easier when you've been friends for a while or have lived together for an extended period of time, others find that its easier to discuss difficult situations with roommates who are closer to strangers or who haven't been living together for more than a few months.

Regardless of your personal preference, having to speak to a roommate about serious or complicated topics is something many people face. Here are some important habits to get into when it comes to preparing and managing difficult conversations in a shared home.

- **Don't Make Ultimatums:** Sometimes in difficult situations, people feel a need to "lay down the law" so to speak and decide to tell their roommate to change their behavior or get out. In reality, this does nothing but make matters worse and is an empty threat unless that person owns the space and put eviction clauses in the roommate's agreement.

o One reason this happens is that people re-act out of anger when there is something that upsets them like finding out their roommate ate food they were saving with-out asking first or left a mess in a common area and is showing no sign of cleaning it up.

o To prevent this from happening, work on keeping your temper in check, if you're someone who struggles with acting impul-sively, and always take at least a few minutes to collect yourself before confront-ing them about whatever has upset you, even wait until the next morning if it is something that can be slept on, to ensure a level head going into the discussion.

- **Don't Make Accusations:** Even if you know that the other person is responsible for creating the situation that is bothering you, simply telling them you know they've done it and that you're not happy about is not a resolution. This type of response guarantees that the roommate will become defensive when confronted and the whole event will result in a negative experience that poisons the living environment, instead of a productive solution that enhances the connection.

  o A better response to situations that upset you and include your roommate is to be open and calmly communicate your feelings with them in a private setting. This can be somewhere in the living space like a kitchen table or living room, but it can also be outside of the home at a coffee shop or somewhere you two have met up before.

- **Don't Let Things Escalate:** If your roommate does something inconsiderate that upsets you, make them aware of it immediately.

  o For example, one day you come home to find your roommate has left their dirty clothes spread out across your shared bathroom floor. You want to speak to them about it, but they won't be home until after you've gone to bed. You're disturbed by the sight of it, but it's the first time it's happened, so you figure maybe they were in a rush or something and will take care of it when they get home. You can ask them about it tomorrow and let them know how it made you feel to come home to such a mess in a shared space.

○ You wake up the next morning to find that the clothes are cleaned up, but your roommate is still in bed and you have to leave for work before they wake up. Since the mess is gone, you decide just to let it go and not think about it again. However, when you come home from work, there are clothes all over the bathroom floor again, and your roommate is gone again.

○ While it bothers you to find the mess, she always has it cleaned by the morning, and due to your conflicting schedules, it is difficult to find a time to talk about it. It continues to happen two to four times a week and after a few months of it, you're about ready to scream.

• Now, instead of a simple "please don't leave dirty clothes in common areas," it has now become a habit, and your roommate has no idea that it is bothering you because you haven't communicated anything about it. So it comes as a surprise when you confront her that may lead to arguments, and further emotional stresses because of poor communication skills.

HOW TO APPROACH DIFFICULT CONVERSATIONS WITH A LANDLORD OR BUILDING SUPERVISOR

Speaking with a landlord or building supervisor can often cause the same kind of dread and stress that comes from having to start a difficult conversation with your boss. While it can be complicated, there are steps to be taken that will help ease the situation and help you feel more prepared for any kind of questions, concerns or arguments they may have about the subject you're bringing up.

The first step to handling any kind of tenant/landlord situation is to be clear about what the issue is that needs to be discussed and check your renter's agreement or specified legal contract that was signed at the start of your tenant/landlord relationship. Is the solution to the problem mentioned in the agreement or does it specify whether the tenant or landlord is responsible for taking care of the matter? These are good questions to have answered before confronting your landlord or discussing something delicate like a recently announced increase in rent or change in policy.

Once you have double-checked the legal terms of your tenant contract, the next step is to reach out to your landlord in a welcoming and inviting manner, even if you are furious over something. Always remember that emotional reactions only lead to further misery for everyone involved. Instead, make sure that you handle planning the conversation with as much professionalism as you would with someone you work with. This approach greatly improves your chances of coming out of any situation with positive thoughts and solutions in hand.

A BASIC CHECKLIST FOR PLANNING & PREPARING TO HAVE DIFFICULT CONVERSATIONS AT HOME

No matter who the conversation is with, if it involves people you see regularly or live with at home, there are some basic questions to ask yourself, rules to keep and tips to follow to make any difficult conversation you have at home as painless and constructive as possible.

- What are my feelings on the subject of the conversation?

  o Is it a reaction coming from an emotional place that may not need to be dealt with through conversational confrontation?

  o Can I control my emotions during a discussion right now or should I give myself more time to center myself before trying to speak with others in the home?

- Keep in mind that maintaining your relationship with the person you live with is the most important goal throughout any difficult situation. Conflicts pass, particularly if you're making an effort to address them, so they don't ooze under the surface of your home life. Relationships with others can be hard to come by in a world where people spend most of their time playing games on their phones.

- Is this conversation one that should be kept in the house or would meeting somewhere public be a better option?

  o Home is supposed to be a haven for everyone, the one place where one can feel safe and uninhibited. If handling a difficult situation is creating tension in the living space, then it may be a good idea to try meeting up for lunch or going for a walk in the park to discuss whatever that has created the need for a difficult conversation.

o   This keeps all parties from developing negative associations with the climate at home, and preserves it as a place of comfort and relaxation when stressful situations can be resolved outside those walls.

•   Don't be afraid to have an outside party present if this is a situation that involves legalities or that may need a mediator.

o   Establish at the beginning of the conversation that the additional party is there simply to be a witness and help calm things down if emotions start to run high, to ensure that you are able to reach a practical solution.

o   Make sure that the person you ask has been properly informed on the situation and the purpose of the conversation that's about to take place.

- o Also, make sure they know that they are not there to take anyone's side and should not become active in the event unless absolutely necessary.

- What options do I have if the conversation does not end how I'm hoping and planning it will?

  - o What are your next steps? Considering this question before having a difficult conversation is not planning for failure, but can help with increasing your confidence for the discussion itself, because you can go in knowing that you have a plan B if this does not work out.

- Establish a timeframe for sharing your concerns at the start of the conversation without being disturbed before opening the floor to questions, comments, and concerns.

o This may not be necessary, it all depends on the specifics of the situation, but it is a good technique to have in mind when you're in charge of starting and leading a difficult conversation at home.

o Let everyone know that they will be heard, but that you need the first five to ten minutes to set up the conversation and lay out the details before everyone starts to discuss it further.

o Depending on the severity of the conversation, you can even go ahead and plan out a set amount of time for everyone to have a chance to speak without interruption. This ensures that everyone has equal speaking time and that even the hardcore introverts in your home know they will be acknowledged.

Chapter 5

HOW TO CALMLY & CONFIDENTLY DIRECT DIFFICULT CONVERSATIONS WITH CHILDREN & FRIENDS

As complex as difficult conversations can be with adults, they can be even more so with children. Situations that call for serious conversations are often emotional and depending on the age of the child, they may not yet have the emotional control skills needed to handle a difficult conversation without escalation or incident.

Like with all stressful situations that require a difficult conversation, it doesn't need to be a painful experience if met with the right approach and handled with the proper delicacy (or directness, depending on the context). In this chapter, we'll provide examples and cover proven methods for speaking clearly and effectively with children in significant situations.

Professional Tip: Clear Your Mind of Expectations for A Smoother Dialogue

This is a professional tip often reserved for comedians practicing their improv skills. Clearing your mind of expectations about how a child is going to behave or respond, verbally or emotionally, during a difficult conversation is critical in managing the tone and the focus of the exchange and achieve your intention.

- Use your empathy skills to try and see the conversation from the child's point of view. This helps with preparation, but it can also hinder your ability to respond immediately and concisely should the child react differently to the responses you were expecting and prepared yourself for.

- Don't let yourself be surprised by different reactions and get held up by not knowing what to say. Keep your mind open and your thoughts clear of solid expectations. Be ready to improvise and mentally prepare yourself for it ahead by learning to accept that no matter how well you plan things out, sometimes you'll need to alter your words and actions on the fly.

- This also makes you more open and accepting to questions they may have that you weren't expecting or that they need to be answered before the conversation can move forward.

THE MOST COMMON "TALKS" ADULTS HAVE WITH CHILDREN & HOW TO PREPARE FOR THEM

Parents are lucky in that they have years to prepare themselves for some of the most difficult conversations anyone can have with anyone and often in a variety of age ranges and emotional experience. Some of the most dreaded conversations adults have to have with children throughout their lives include:

- **Introducing & Explaining Puberty:** The topics needing to be covered with this difficult conversation are vastly different for boys and girls. Children receiving this talk are just starting to experience uncontrollable emotional changes and physical changes in their body that they have little to no previous knowledge of. Depending on how old the child in question is, this conversation could have a tone of preparation to it (letting the child know what to expect just as or even before puberty starts) or it can have a strictly educational tone (for children receiving the talk after they've started their pubescent phase).

- **Covering Upsetting News & Events:** These conversations can be impossible to prepare for but can be handled with the same basic con-

versation guidelines used for handling unexpected situations at work.

o Parents with younger children often have
  extra time to collect their thoughts and also
  to control how much their child is exposed
  to these kinds of news.

o Parents with middle and high school-aged
  children can have difficulties since they
  have easy access to the news on their
  phones throughout the day while the parents may not have heard anything since
  they've been busy at work all day.

• **Discussing Death & Loss:** These are tough
  topics to cover with anyone, but it is especially
  true when discussing them with children. With
  adults, difficult conversations about death and
  loss are typically delivering to someone who already understands the severity and of the situation. With children, it is most likely that they

have not experienced a major loss and depending on their age, may not even know what death is.

These are just a few examples of the types of conversations parents and adults who work closely with children have to prepare themselves for. Regardless of the topic itself, there are a few tips and tricks that can be useful as the time for each discussion comes up:

- **Patience, Patience, Patience**: As adults speaking to children, it is always important to remember that your emotional control skills and understanding of the larger world are much more advanced than a child's of any age. They do not yet have the experience and skills necessary to keep from getting emotional or asking a million questions that you don't think needs to be explained.

  o If you are emotional or in a state where your patience may be thinner than normal, it is better to temporarily put the discussion on hold and give yourself time to calm down before getting involved in a detailed, possibly life-altering, conversation with a child.

o Even if the conversation is being held because of negative behavior on the child's part that needs to be addressed, remaining calm and speaking without frustration is critical in handling these types of situations with children.

• **Be Clear About Your Intentions from the Jump:** If the conversation is about explaining something major like a natural disaster or a plane crash to a child, then it is imperative to set the right kind of tone. You would not want to lure them into a sense of joy and playfulness before dropping the bombshell. This teaches children to be hesitant and doubtful of happy activities as they may be nothing more than a cover for bad news to come.

o   Whatever the context of the conversation, make sure that the setting, tone, language and visible body language are appropriate for the task. Children are impressionable and can be easily confused by difficult conversations, so it comes down to the adult to make sure the environment and the atmosphere are clean and correct.

- **Choose Your Words Carefully & Stay Focused on the Issue at Hand:** The kind of language you use can make all the difference in how smoothly a difficult conversation goes. When it comes to children, the best course of action is to stick to simple phrases and direct answers. It is sometimes tempting to try and dance around the issue in order to make the setting less awkward or make the conversation move along more quickly.

o It can be easy to get distracted when discussing important issues with children because people seek out reasons to change the subject when things start to get strained or stressful. This does nothing but creating more confusion on the part of the child and more burden on the adults as it ends up drawing out the conversation, or ultimately bringing it to an end without covering all of the topics that needed to be discussed.

o One of the most common techniques for successful handling difficult conversations with children is to follow these steps:

- Open with a brief explanation of what the conversation will be covering and why it is necessary.

- From there, list any concerns or issues you want them to discuss openly with you. It could be about behavior at school, questions they asked you previously that you were unprepared to answer at the time or any other number of themes.

- Once you have made your intention clear and explained the specifics of what you are expecting from the conversation, use the rest of the time to focusing on their questions, concerns or opinions on the topic.

- Listen carefully and respond with answers that are straightforward and educational.

- Be careful to monitor your tone as "educational" can sometimes come off as patronizing instead, and cause offense or make the child reluctant to ask further questions.

- **Make Sure to Finish the Conversation:** This seems like common sense, but when it comes to having discussions with children on problematic subjects it can be tempting to look for an easy out in order to escape a difficult situation. Instead, always make sure that discussions with children (particularly the major ones) end with an evaluation of what you both spoke about and what was learned or uncovered during the talk. Ask one last time about any questions they may still have and make sure to ask any of your own.

  o Another good practice is to let the children know that even though the conversation is over, they can always bring up new questions or concerns afterward.

- ▪ This helps to build trust between you and the child you're speaking with and also encourages more activity and open conversation in future discussions.

- **Ask for Help:** With how easy it is for children to be confused or affected by the things they see and hear, never hesitate to seek out assistance when you are feeling unprepared, inexperienced or overwhelmed by a difficult conversation that you need to have with a child.

Professional Tip: When in Doubt, Take to Social Media!

While it does present some challenges for parents with older children, one of the best things about being a parent in the 21st century is the access to information, and instant search results that come with having the internet and social sites always carried around in our pockets. By simply searching Facebook or Twitter for parent-focused communities, anyone can ask their personal questions and seek advice on any child-related topic with just a few clicks. Search engines provide access to child care blogs and websites that are run by experienced parents and active followers that are happy to share their knowledge on any number of topics.

If you are a first-time parent or just someone who feels more comfortable with a second opinion from others who have struggled with the same issues, there are endless resources available on social media sites that you are most likely already a member of. Use those resources to help develop your parenting and communication skills whenever you need help!

DIFFICULT CONVERSATIONS THROUGHOUT THE YEARS: DIFFERENT AGE GROUPS, DIFFERENT APPROACHES

The guidelines listed above are a good start for preparing yourself to speak with children of any age, but it is good to acknowledge and understand that different age ranges react distinctively to different approaches.

Here is a closer look at some of the most popular methods in practice for having difficult discussions with children of all ages:

- **Toddlers & Preschoolers to Early Elementary School Children (2 to 5 Years Old)**

  o With any luck, difficult conversations with children of this age are few and far between. They are not involved in the most up-to-date news or talking to people about topics that would be better suited for older children and adults.

  o Keep all conversations with children of this age to the point, making sure to open by asking what they already know about the topic being covered. Don't offer too much information that they may not yet fully understand which can lead to more questions that may not be directly related to the issue.

o Make sure to keep language simple and plain, especially when describing people or ideas and talking about emotions.

▪ Children of this age also do not have a vast emotional vocabulary or the experience to start developing one. So instead of using words like "stressful" or "frustrating", stick to words like "sad" and "mad" that you won't have to spend a lot of time trying to explain.

o Focus on making them feel safe and let them know that they don't need to be frightened or worried about difficult events or changes. Reassure them that as an adult, you and other adults are the ones who will handle the situation.

• **Late Elementary & Middle School Ages (6 to 13 Years Old)**

o Parents and adults are more likely to start

getting their real practice by having diffi-cult conversations with children of this age. By the time children reach this age they are proficiently reading and writing which means they have the potential to receive in-formation from just about anywhere they look.

- Now that they are out of the house more, many children of this age also have their own phone with limited ac-cess to social media and other sites where they can be exposed to a stressful or upsetting situation without any prep-aration from their parents beforehand.

- Due to this early exposure to complex situations, many children of this age are also already learning how to form their own opinions and are capable of talking back and arguing when adults try to discuss things seriously with them.

o With children of this age range, it is important to focus discussions on emotional responses and personal thoughts.

- Instead of just asking what they think about the situation being covered, make sure to ask them how they feel about it and what kind of actions they are considering for dealing with it. Doing this as a part of regular conversations with children helps teach them from an early age the difference between actions that are driven by thoughts and actions that are impulsive responses to emotional stress.

o This is also the age range where children start to really explore their curiosity and have less hesitation about asking every question that pops into their head. While this can make preparing for a serious discussion challenging, it also helps with expanding your child's view of the world and helping you get a firmer grasp of their perspective on how their life in general and personal views are changing.

- **Late Middle School & High School Teenagers (14 to 18 Years Old)**

    o Speak to children in this age range as you would speak to another adult. Teenagers are rebellious, emotional and constantly confused about the developments happening in their mind and body, as well as the potentially distressing situations they are exposed to on a daily basis.

        ▪ While as an adult you already know that the teenage emotional experience is limited compared to that of parents, teachers, and counselors, many teenagers see themselves as adults already and can easily become defensive or obstinate if they feel like they're beating patronized.

o Be encouraging about expressing their thoughts and opinions in an unhindered and confident manner. These are the years where children acquire and exercise their communication skills and may not have many opportunities outside the home to do so. This is why it is so important to insist on an active dialogue where both of you can ask questions, and both of you are expected to answer honestly.

▪ One of the easiest ways to build trust with teenage children and earn their respect at the same time is to openly admit when you do not have the skills or the information needed to answer their questions or explain a complex situation.

- This encourages honesty and shows the child you're speaking to that adults are just people too. Describing this to them and having them experience it for themselves in a positive aspect is one of the benefits of swallowing your pride and leveling the field. It also gives you the chance to ask if you can talk about it tomorrow or later in the day after you've had a chance to do some research, gather some information or ask some questions of your own.

OUTSIDE THE FAMILY, BUT EQUALLY IMPORTANT TO YOU: HAVING DIFFICULT CONVERSATIONS WITH FRIENDS

Speaking to people outside of the workplace or family, whether you know them or not, is often easier for people than having to bring up difficult topics with people they see and interact with daily. While this is not always the case, there are definitely different approaches that can be taken when having to speak with good friends or perfect strangers about difficult subjects or problematic behaviors.

In this section, we will be covering widely practiced techniques and approaches, as well as providing some valuable tips from a variety of sources on how to deal with difficult conversations no matter how close you are to the person you need to speak with.

The Methods to Mastering Difficult Topics with Close Friends & People You Know

Conversations with friends and relations are supposed to be fun, exciting and entertaining compared to our daily work and school lives. There are times in every friendship though where a difficult conversation must be held, and it is vital to maintaining your relationship that you have the knowledge and skills needed to handle the situation without incident.

Some of the difficult conversations people have with their friends include:

- Discussing new habits or behaviors that are either concerning and need to be addressed or acknowledging positive behaviors and celebrating all progress they've made to get away from a former state of distress.

- Talking to them about personal issues that may make them uncomfortable or something you just haven't discussed with them before.

- Delivering bad news like having witnessed their significant other in a precarious situation or telling them you're going to have to move for work.

Some of the most effective practices and fundamentals to keep in mind when planning a difficult conversation with a friend include:

- Make sure to open the conversation on a positive note, by thanking your friend for taking the time to talk with you. If they feel appreciated from the beginning of the conversation, they are more likely to be open, responsive and active throughout the rest of the talk so that you can work together, and both come to a resolution that benefits everyone.

  o Don't forget to be open about your feelings, letting your friend know how much you value your relationship and being honest about any anxieties or concerns you have about even bringing up a sensitive subject.

- Instead of starting by immediately bringing up your issues or questions, conversations with friends work best with a more inquisitive tactic.

o Start by asking your friend if there is anything in their personal life that they may not have shared, but that may be affecting them more than they realize.

o If they ask why, bring up your concerns such as a behavioral change or that you've been seeing them less and that they're staying home more. Anything you talk about, do so without judgment and with sympathy. It is possible that something is deeply troubling them and they have just been looking for an opportunity to bring it up.

• Be sure to wrap it up on a positive note and move forward from there, letting them know that anything they shared is safe with you and that they can always come to you when something is troubling them.

Regardless of their age or their relationship to you, there are always steps that can be taken and proven approaches that work best for each group when it comes to having difficult conversations. Just keep in mind:

- Everyone wants to feel like they are valued and respected, even young people who are just starting to experience a world of difficulties and how they should be handled.

- Speak to anyone you need to with the same kind of tone and language that you would expect to receive; angry outbursts and hurtful reactions only further damage relationships (personal or professional).

Difficult conversations should never be responsible for creating or escalating emotional tension or ending a relationship with a friend or anyone you are close to. Remember your guidelines, develop your skills and always make it your priority to listen, understand and acknowledge the thoughts and feelings of anyone you speak with going forward.

Chapter 6

HOW TO ALWAYS BE PREPARED FOR UNEXPECTED SITUATIONS ON THE FLY

Ideally, all difficult conversations will not have to be untaken without ample time to prepare. Unfortunately, life just doesn't work that way, and there will always be times where stressful situations arise without warning and need to be dealt with immediately. These situations do not have to escalate into emotional outbursts, be pushed aside and avoided until they become much larger issues or be dreaded as anxiety-inducing nightmares.

It all comes down to having the knowledge and skills necessary to manage and respond to difficult situations when they happen or when they need to be handled. This chapter will explore some of the more detailed techniques to handling unexpected situations along with examples and some powerful tips for mastering the art of remaining calm and in charge, regardless of what the day may throw at you!

ALWAYS READY FOR ACTION: LEARNING HOW TO HANDLE UNEXPECTED SITUATIONS WITH EASE & COOL COLLECTION

We learn from a young age that life is unpredictable and that situations can develop out of seemingly nowhere, throwing a wrench into the workings of our daily activities.

It sounds like a contradiction, but the key to success throughout life (and in any endeavor) is to prepare yourself for the unexpected. This is not always possible, but in the cases of difficult conversations, there is often some kind of building issue or previous action that has led to the development of this situation in the first place.

The first step to doing this is to accept that unexpected events are going to happen and while you can prepare as much as you want, there will be times when a situation comes up without warning and requires attention. In these situations, you may not be able to control the event or the reactions of any other people involved, but you do have the ability to control your own responses. This is where successfully being able to respond to change becomes an invaluable life skill, and once you've accepted the unexpected, you can start gathering information on different methods of leading difficult conversations and putting them into practice!

Some beneficial tips and techniques to mastering the ability to keep control of difficult situations with unexpected occurrences include:

- **Don't Let It Get You Down:** Anxiety and concern are natural responses to unexpected developments, but if allowed to dominate your thoughts for too long before handling a difficult situation, they can be detrimental to making progress and creating solutions.

o It is easier said than actually accomplished, but keeping a positive outlook is the best way to keep negative emotions in check. You've accepted that you can't control or change things that happen suddenly, now it is just a matter of remaining confident in your own abilities to lead and steer difficult conversations in the direction of positive adjustments.

- **Plan for the Best:** It is not enough to just keep a positive attitude, it also helps to plan for the best resolution possible for the situation!

  o Try to expect the best outcome before starting a difficult conversation since it helps with controlling your responses by clearing your mind, allowing you to think clearly and make confident decisions on how to move forward each time something new occurs.

o The best outcome may not always be what occurs, but knowing what your preferred outcome would have been will keep your specific goals in mind throughout the conversation.

- Use your reserved daily reflection time to ponder over what occurred and what could have been handled differently to achieve your desired result.

- If the actual conclusion to the conversation was a better resolution than you expected, think about how that idea was brought up or how you and the others participating reacted as the option was discussed.

- **Trust Yourself & Your Abilities**: Even if you're new to having difficult conversations (especially when there isn't time to fully prepare), it is important to have faith in your decisions and trust in the steps you're going to take.

  o Self-confidence is one of the most desirable traits searched for in leaders and managers. Learning about and practicing the skills needed to handle unexpected situations is something that professionals, parents, councilors and nearly anyone else you could think of can benefit from as experienced.

- **Gather Yourself Before Reacting**: One way to control emotional responses to unexpected happenings is to make sure that (even if it is something that needs to be handled promptly) you take a moment to remove yourself from the situation, clear your thoughts and make sure you have a clear goal for the conversation and know what you want to say before interacting with others.

o This ensures that not only you but the others who have just learned of the unexpected circumstance have a moment to get control of their thoughts and feelings so that the issue can be discussed peacefully, productively and without outbursts.

Professional Tip: Keep Your Calm & Find Your Center

Remaining calm in the face of conflict, interruptions and unexpected situations that arise without warning is the key to leading and participating in any successful conversation. Psychologists, business professionals and others who study communication or find themselves having difficult conversations as part of their daily lives, encourage everyone to find a way to keep in control of their emotions when these situations come up.

- **Give Meditation A Chance**: Even though some difficult conversations come with no time to prepare, it is usually possible to get a few minutes to yourself before the start of a complex or dreaded conversation. Meditation is a powerful exercise with a variety of benefits and uses that can assist with maintaining a collected mind throughout nearly any kind of situation.

  o Ask to be excused for a few minutes and find somewhere quiet (or in the open air) in order to collect your thoughts. Close your eyes, breathe deeply and rhythmically, in and out.

  o Take control of any anxiety or negative emotions that may be clouding your thoughts and expel them from your mind.

Meditation is different for everybody, so it may take trying a few techniques before you are able to find one (or a combination of them) that works for you.

○ Some people like to have a physical talisman or trinket to hold onto. They hold it in their palm or move it between their fingers while they reflect. The pressure of a solid object can be comforting, especially for those who have trouble focusing on their own.

○ Others like to have calming music on their phone in order to always have it with them if they need a quick calming session.

• **Develop Personalized Affirmations:** These are powerful calming and meditating tools. Affirmations are short statements or quotes that are repeated (mentally or aloud) or concentrated on for a set amount of time in order to focus and center your thoughts. They are good tools for handling any kind of stressful situation the day may throw at you and can be developed to address emotional issues that you face on a regular basis.

o   Examples of affirmations that can help when difficult conversations come out of nowhere include:

- I am calm. I am in control.

- I am focused. I am centered.

- Exhale stress. Inhale peace.

- My thoughts matter. My ideas are strong.

o   If these affirmations don't work for you, it is easy to come up with your own!

- Ask yourself what causes you stress or what stimulates your anxiety.

- Once identified, you can choose a statement that focuses on each specific issue.

o Once you have your chosen affirmations, explore using them in different ways to calm your mind and emotions.

- Some people close their eyes and repeat the phrase until they reach the emotional or mental state intended. This can be done out loud or silently, depending on which works best for the individual.

- Others like to write out their affirmations. Some write it out once on a blank piece of paper and then make doodles around the phrase while thinking on it. Some prefer to write it over and over, preferring the visual of writing it out instead of repeating it verbally or mentally.

THE IMPORTANCE OF LEARNING TO HANDLE UNEXPECTED CHANGES IN ESTABLISHED ORGANIZATIONS

The following example is a common occurrence in the business world that most people find themselves having to deal with (as a leader or a team member) at least once throughout their professional lives.

One difficult conversation that is often delegated to supervisors or team leaders from higher level employees and typically needs to be handled without a lot of warning is telling your office team (or any group of professionals working together) that the company is understaffed, and everyone is expected to pick up some of the extra work until new hires can be brought in and trained.

No one likes hearing that they are going to have extra work on a daily basis so how the announcement is approached can make all the difference in how the team responds. If you find yourself the one that has to manage the situation, the first step to take is to make sure you get all of your questions answered by whoever it is that made the decision and that you know the details of the situation and what has led to this. You may not always be able to get straight answers depending on the conduct of the company and the specifics of the situation, but it is important to remember that any questions you have for them will most likely be asked of you by your employees or co-workers during the conversation to come.

The next step is to look at the situation from the perspective of the other employees. Ask yourself the following questions:

- How upset will the team be about this announcement? How can I ease their stress and emotional changes caused by this unexpected change?

- What kind of language should I use to be as clear and sympathetic as possible?

- What kind of questions will they ask and how will I respond?

  o Anticipating questions and concerns before holding a meeting or delivering bad news can help make any situation run more smoothly. It helps give leaders a chance to practice empathy while also assessing what information they possess and what information they still need to get based on how they feel their team members will react.

Once you have answered these questions and feel more confident in your ability to keep control of the situation, the final step is to come up with at least one or two options for how to best resolve the issue. Making an effort to come up with a basic solutions shows the team that you are also actively involved in the situation, and once these solutions have been shared, you can then open the floor to see what other questions, concerns, and resolutions the team can come up with together.

Professional Tip: Know Who to Contact in Desperate Situations

Having a list or a collection of helpful resources is always a good plan, no matter what kind of situation you find yourself dealing with. These resources could include supervisors or managers that serve as a mentor, peers or friends that are experienced with what you happen to be dealing with right now (such as calling other parents you trust for advice when needed). It could also include emergency numbers and hotlines for those who find themselves dealing with highly emotional or psychological issues, like doctors and councilors handling unexpected developments with their patients.

When it comes down to it, never be afraid to ask for help. It saves everyone time and increases productivity when people who are underprepared or do not feel qualified to handle the task they have been given are open about their concerns. This opens up the opportunity to more quickly agreed upon and effective resolutions from people who are more knowledgeable or experienced on the issue at hand. This is where the ability to delegate is a valuable skill if it is necessary for managing the unexpected situation, also the ability to assess developments and make decisions on how best to proceed.

A BASIC CHECKLIST FOR DEALING WITH UNEXPECTED DEVELOPMENTS & MAINTAINING COMPLETE CONTROL

This checklist can be used to enhance the basic Difficult Conversations Checklist you've developed through experience or research. The following questions address thoughts and feelings specifically regarding unexpected events and how to best handle them when they occur.

- Did you ask any questions you had about the situation when initially presented with it?

- o Make sure you have all of the information you need before making decisions or bringing people of differing opinions on the subject together for a difficult conversation.

- Do you have all of the information you need to handle the situation effectively?

  - o Have you looked at all sides and arguments that will (or could) be discussed? Are you prepared for how you'll respond?

- How did you initially respond to the news of an unexpected issue? Was it appropriate for the situation?

  - o Monitor changes in your feelings and behaviors as the situation unfolds and think about how you can improve reactions you could have handled better or encourage positive reactions that helped things progress.

- How will this unexpected change affect how things stand in your current environment?

    o Could this be a positive development or will there be the potential for additional stress?

- Is there anything that has recently happened that could have helped predict this or anything that could have been done to prevent this?

    o These are not thoughts that are good to dwell on should the situation turn negative, but they are good to contemplate when reviewing a situation and deciding how to best move forward.

- Do you feel safe in the current setting and welcomed to share your thoughts and feelings with others involved?

    o Use your personal emotional control, centering and grounding methods to gain command of your responses and reactions before letting yourself get overwhelmed, frustrated or offended.

- After a difficult conversation, how do you think about the situation?

  o Did you handle yourself how you would expect others to behave in the same situation?

  o Are you thinking about where the subject was left off after the discussion, or are you thinking about the future based on all of the progress made during the session?

    ▪ One sign that a difficult conversation was not handled well or fully resolved is if you or others involved are focused on the past and what has happened instead of what is happening or needs to be done. This is where understanding the difference between reflecting and obsessing becomes important.

What other questions can you think of that will be helpful in keeping you prepared and determined to succeed in stressful situations that may come your way? Use the checklists contained in this book as guidelines but never forget that developing these skills is a lifelong process, so you should never be afraid to add, pick or choose which methods that work best for you!

While unexpected situations can be frustrating and awkward, it is also good to keep in mind that just because something was not predicted or prepared for, it doesn't mean that it is a bad thing. Sometimes unexpected changes can lead to positive influences that would not have been possible if the conversation had gone as originally planned. This may not always be the case, but it is always good to keep an open mind, listening when others have contradicting opinions or creative ideas, even if it something you initially disagree with or do not want to hear.

CONCLUSION

No matter what your individual goals are, hopefully you now have the necessary information you need to turn it into actionable tools that makes mastering difficult conversations anywhere manageable (if not, even a pleasant) experience for everyone involved.

Knowing how to speak to people in any given situation is a valuable skill that can be put to good use in any industry for those hoping to build a professional career, or to strengthen bonds with family and friends for those looking for more personal uses.

Thank you for purchasing this book on handling difficult conversations throughout life! Good luck in all your future endeavors and never stop learning!

And one last thing, please consider leaving a review on Amazon to share your thoughts of this book.

amazon.com/review/create-review/listing

www.ingramcontent.com/pod-product-compliance
Lightning Source LLC
Chambersburg PA
CBHW072142170526
45158CB00004BA/1468